Breaking the Surface

Ian Reid

Breaking the Surface

Breaking the Surface
ISBN 978 1 76109 620 4
Copyright © text Ian Reid 2023
Cover image: Ian Reid

First published 2023 by
Ginninderra Press
PO Box 3461 Port Adelaide 5015
www.ginninderrapress.com.au

Contents

Ruffled Edges
 Wherever the body is 11
 Shifty shorelines 14
 Stranded 17
 The past as a basin: West Head 18
 The present as a basin: Collaroy 19
 Yallingup after a year 20
 Long after landfall 21
 Loving on the edge 22
 Stone or shell 23
 Slipway lament 24
 Coming up again 25

Riffled Pages
 A beginning 29
 A prospect 30
 An exchange 31
 May 32
 Either way 33
 Being drawn 34
 Coming to a sudden corner 35
 Growing like topsy, it goes like turvy 36
 Restorative 37
 Escapologists 38
 Revenant 39
 Spring nuptials 40
 Coming to our senses 41

Perching Ghosts
 On your bike, Wordsworth! 45
 Elsewhere, elsewhen 48

Hanging on	51
The Baths	52
The Swamp	53
Chums' Club	54
Bubblegumption	56
In over your head	57
Small print	58
Alfred Crusoe, apartment #8	60
Zero	62
Evening out	63
Walhalla	64
Finally	65
Reprieved	66
Cured	67
Blank desertion	68
A goose, too, is a bird of poetry	69
Dogged by Sirius	70
A traction	71
Reclamation	72
Breathless	73

Filial Shadows

So long	77
Chip to old block	79
The coat	80
Ticker	81
On the wharf	82
The company of milk	83
A pencilled message	84
Our Pelorus	85
Foxhill	86
Catching up	87

What's in a name?	88
Matrimonial trigonometry	90
Restricted entry	91
Longingly in longhand	94
Thrifty optimism	95
All thumbs	96
Ageing	98

Speaking Pictures

Simmo's aphorism	101
Never satisfied with seeing	102
Watering the land	103
Vital signs	104
Hanging in the Discharge Lounge	106
Silk on cinnabar	107
Somnambulist	108
Stony silence	109
Incident on table 4	110
A hooded boat	111
Amphibious	112
Not so black and white	113
Dead, naked in the looking glass	114

Other Bodies

Sea-changes	117
Be careful what you fish for	119
Out of place	120
Bathos at Balyang	122
My migrant way of moving	124
Being loved to bits	126
The cat's whiskers	127
Turnings	128
Reciprocal mysteries	129

In a darkening shade	130
Filth into growth	132
De profundis	134
Acknowledgements	135
About the author	137

Ruffled Edges

Wherever the body is

As rain falls hard on the military funeral
(ashes to slush, sods to silt)
President Umbrella tells those who're stiff
to attention
Americans will never forget lives lost to protect
freedom in Iraq, Afghanistan,
wherever.

They believe that's true in a country where
extinction is never seen as final.
They believe it because their mighty eagle
even when almost expunged from skies
figures unflappably on every greenback.
They believe it because at the local stadium
a hundred thousand voices cheer the Wolverines
whose originals buckled to bullets decades ago.
Museums call this kind of history natural
and so it seems to people totally stuffed
with memory, still gorging out on hope.
Witness a sign in a truckers' roadside café:
GOD, GUNS AND GUTS MADE THIS COUNTRY –
LET'S KEEP IT THAT WAY.
Witness another, beside a suburban chapel:
WHEREVER THE BODY IS,
THERE WILL THE EAGLES GATHER.

Easy to mock, but where do you stand to say 'they'?
What's your position?

Consider a creature of the French Pacific,
its freely amphibious life: how enviable
to be in your element not only here but there!
Yet nobody yearns for the stranded end of longing.
Imagine turning turtle, turning under
the bluest of enfolding waters, waiting
for darkness near this nickel island coast
before breaking the surface,
tottering ashore, gut-lumbered,
labouring on up the gritty slope
driven by a birth clock's tick
into sudden lights, a shudder, an overturning,
poles, ropes, shouts, a butchering knife.
Changes places now,
stand over here, and say in the flare of morning –
that blade hammered in between the belly plates,
is it theirs or yours, and whose
are the thick blood bubbles, the ripped-out eggs?

On a hill near that same bay, a memorial graveyard
for misplaced servicemen from the old Pacific War.
Pacific they are these days: gravel keeps them that way.
The slab lines curve like a great bird's gathering wing,
and each name is listed, wherever the body is.

Snapshot exotica? Not so entirely remote,
those grey souvenirs, from your own collective presumptions.
Here are you; there are corpses.
'They' and 'we' have no place.
Wherever the body is,
the plural's too large an umbrella.

The opening lines refer to Arlington National Cemetery in the USA. The graves depicted later in the poem are those of New Zealand soldiers within a war cemetery in Bourail, New Caledonia, located near the Baie des Tortues, where I once saw a large turtle killed by local Kanak people for their food.

Shifty shorelines

Line of shore
the single thing it made of him
this line of shore.
– Barry Hill

High seas are on the move again – not sudden
stormy surges, but a slow deepening flood
that laps now at new levels of old lives,
submerging bluffs, seeping up valley floors,
refilling stranded gorges with the stealth
of a swollen grudge, ruthless in search of reasons.

People rise differently to this occasion
or slouch indifferently, as the case may be.
Some disregard the forecasts altogether.
The seals, giant sea-garden swayback slugs,
are curling over the Kaikoura rocks
while seagulls, loutish, loud bodgie patrols
loiter on beaches where futures loll in the shallows.

But the change is too insidious for those
who like a crisis to be grand, and Messrs
Canute and Gilgamesh are with us always.
Off stomps a former friend – looks a bit like you? –
making a fist of resentment, to punch at the sand.
Loyalty drains. Runnels of rage rush in.
The line that is being redrawn singles him out.

Those dreams of inundation, all the swirling
angular bodies… Where did the children go?
PROCEED WITH (says the sign) – and someone's hand
has crossed out CAUTION, substituted HAVOC!
Head fast, headfirst, for the highest ground.

In Wellington, when southerlies rip and wrench
at the window in this bay above the harbour
while spiders crouch half-pissed behind the soap,
it's time to run up the hill that's like a flag.
Cobwebs blow away as you open the door
and your blood goes dancing a zigzag path to hope.
But what can you see from the summit? Are you lost?

Sydney: wake to the glare through a moonlit window
and hear the creaky sound of a yacht's rig stretch –
yet the house is miles inland, and no wind stirs.
But look! There it goes: the small spinnakered vessel
over this placid, vertical sea: a snail
pressing against the glass on a long traverse
in some unmapped but not unknown direction.

Along the lunar margins of the Swan
at Applecross, dark nets are cast for prawns
while talking heads are bobbing on the current.
The moon draws all the fluid through its gills
and lifts the ripples to a nearby room
that glows with light, vein-latticed, from the red
sac of an egg in water, floating up.

Everything flows: you can't step twice into
the same old reverie. Even the dregs that seem
immobilised by regret are on the move.
Peer closely at an outline of your past,
a huge old hulk, embedded in all the grit
and slime of the tidal rim: quite changeless? No.
It goes on rotting, turning into sludge
that feeds a thousand parasites each meal.

Reaching this coast has taken all your life
so far. The purple trees give calm relief.
You've come to where the jacaranda smile
merges with ruffled edges of the real.

Stranded

Though dice keep foaming beside your feet as you move
away from the squint of sun over ground gritpacked
with minute and discreet undertakings, you don't yet pay
attention to all that flicker; and strolling over
the floor of one world, you forget it's roofing another
as you point at patterned relief where water withdraws
after plaiting the sand like a loafcrust, out there too
as clouds puff up from somewhere on that yeasty horizon –
till you turn inwards, leaving the strand behind,
along the grey estuary's bubbleflecked edge: here comes
a bleak mood sidelong, bordering on mishap, and you walk
among scumsmeared fishbody flotsam. Something unsaid
tightens the air, and is gutting the years underneath you.

That's when some father or foetus slips off your shoulder
to vanish with a last quick breath. You're peering down
one of those splinterthin shafts near your feet
but your love, unpausing, is already far up the beach
forgetful of tides.

The past as a basin: West Head

A long and steep descent: he picks his way
as gravel shifts underfoot, trivial fret
pestering each downward step. It's not a day

when spirits lift, or wincing bones forget
their brittle history of injuries,
or even love can be discharged of debt.

This beach now: wave-crimped light seems keen to please
and there's a flourish in those frothy suds,
but he sits sullenly, chin on his knees,

and listens to the chug of heavy blood.
You watch old chaps row dinghies to and fro
and boys dig worms up from the estuary mud,

then coax him into walking. On your slow
amble along the shore you hear the call
of some bleak seagull; then it's time to go.

As you return now, he still tries to haul
his shadow – moody laggard – up the slope,
lugging its swollen legs, long arms, and small

diminished head. Hard not to give up hope
of severing what ties him to that grey
drear umbrage. Which of you could slash the rope?

The present as a basin: Collaroy

Past a tide-rinsed rock-edged pool where the old still play
at being young as ever, here you roam
along this grainy rim of that same bay

where your teen selves would skip, and dreams float home
like food from some wrecked yacht, doing a loop
with sepia wave-twirled sea-fronds in the foam.

By reef and palm, today's a golden scoop
as wishfulness comes inshore with a rush
to fill you up again. You're cock-a-hoop!

You kick your heels up, caper over trash
that lies discarded on the glittering sand:
fish-heads with gills like crimson bottlebrush.

Around the corner, long rock-layers extend
in filo tessellation, launching pads
to kingdom come, or roads to a vanished end

forgotten by these lolling mums and dads
who cover half the beach with picnic gear,
towels, lotions, sunhats for their little tads –

taking you back into a fretful year
long before you could breathe this open air
of shared contentment, intimate as fear.

Yallingup after a year

Last time your gaze was fixed on the bursting sea.
As if deferring to your element,
you sat near the foam and stared into the spray.

Easy to have overlooked this marker,
half-covered with a hedge, remembering
some boy drowned out there. The waves get bleaker.

Easy to have overlooked these weeds
along beach paths. Now the warm smell of fennel
reminds you of walks with parents down dead roads.

One land's edge leads your mind towards another.
But still the coast here, oldest on the planet,
is new to you. Could be a foster father?

Long after landfall

Friday, on the beach – but the single footprint
is your own, filling slowly with foamy water
that may have slipped past Island Bay
or slopped around Banks Peninsula
on its way here to seep into these toe-marks.

Easier to have made the Tasman crossing
than to find your balance ashore.
Scuffing through shifty water margins
you know it's time to admit
that long after landfall there's no assurance
of having both feet on this or any ground.
Just half your toes make an impression here.

You paddle over pebbles, bones of contentment
sucked at by sea lip: gleaming, outlandish
till waves withdraw, leave them to sun and sand.
Lustre drains away. They are dingy stones.
Belonging is an elementary matter.
Longing is what's left. It's on the ebb.

Loving on the edge

One way of being at the beach
is to stand there watching
wishes roil and swell,
foam up, fall back,
and seeing how the sand
beckons yet repels each pulse
in an endless teasing.

Another is to pick a path
through stroll towards frolic,
feeling your way
beyond the flags
and the safety of footwear
as motion that leads to dancing
starts with tiptoe paddling.

Or there's running beside the tide
towards the rocks, not knowing whether
sea and self will converge
or veer apart,
nor whether the water's rush
will set you afloat or suck you under
as the race gushes faster.

And when it's all subsiding
there's a fainter sound, naked
as a pillow-muffled whisper:
'I thought you'd never make it.'

Stone or shell

Under the water, you'd hardly tell them apart:
both round-gleaming, seeming sound.
On the sand, sun-dried, they alter.

Now you see that the stone is far too hard
for protecting anything beyond
itself, but the shell is a shelter:

within it, like a blood rush through the heart
or a panting dog homeward bound,
inner waves run helter-skelter.

Slipway lament

Coffee Point Boatyard: this was once a berth
for paddle steamers after they had crossed
the Swan, tight packed with picnickers from Perth –
a place to take your time. But it's long lost.
Jetties have come and gone. Now nothing slides
over the slipway trace, except dull sand
and shapeless water pushed or pulled by tides.
Little is left of so much that was planned.
Here you remain in limbo. That faint sound
of something moving – like a paddle wheel? –
was just the ghost of hope. You wait around
in vain as light grows dim and wishes keel.
Cold air drifts into corners of the bay.
No one will come. All boats have turned away.

In 1896, Alexander Matheson, businessman and politician, invested in real estate on the southern side of Perth's Swan River near its junction with the Canning, subdividing the suburb of Applecross and building a jetty and boatyard at Coffee Point to support the venture. The envisaged development did not prosper in his time.

Coming up again

You've seen it, probably done it, often enough:
an underwater swirl, the upward rush
of a swimmer surfacing, starburst of spray
and then a sudden sucking in of breath.

But a rising body may emerge perhaps
too late to gasp for air – as when at Esthwaite
a pile of unclaimed clothes drew a silent crowd
to witness the upsurge of that ghastly corpse.

Sooner or later, water gives up each ghost.
The surface is too fragile to keep them down.
Wronged friends, submerged lapses or sunken selves
appear, bolt upright, from your long-drowned past.

The incident at Esthwaite Water in England's Lake District is the one described by Wordsworth in Book 5 of 'The Prelude'.

Riffled Pages

A beginning

Okains Bay, Banks Peninsula

Would it seem later like opening a dance, a book?

She turned with a lift of her shoulder. He shifted his feet
towards and away, until the old cave swung up
into line behind her, and then the toppling hill
and the tipsy posts of the jetty.
He sidled closer, glancing across at those eyes
past which the wind, insistent as fantasy,
kept shuffling strands of her hair. She shook her head
at what – an obliqueness of sunlight?
Was she losing her balance? Was he finding his tongue?

His foot was tapping the sand. Her smile tapped his desire.
The beach had become a floor to spin upon.
Cave, hill and jetty began to take their measure,
slow, slow, quickquick slow, her fingers keeping time
at a cool arm's length. His gesture circled a cliché.
The sea riffled pages of pleasure.
For the moment much seemed possible, if unlikely.
Would she read him from step to step?
Would he dance her from cover to cover?

A prospect

Church Point, Northern Beaches

Look up from your pumpkin soup through this future window
where sunlight hopscotches towards your upstairs room
across a marina tingling with possibilities.
Just below, young dogs are out on jetty patrol:
such to and fro! Smelling old salts, they've caught
a whiff of embarkation. Over there
it's hard to tell what's island, what's peninsula,
where you might harvest cucurbits or harbour hopes.

You're not sure what to make of the slouching hills,
their silhouetted heaviness. You look away.
But later, picking your way between the plates
of jellyfish, zigzagging past sandcastles
smashed in childhood, you see on every side
the gaps, the nooks, the inlets of your need.

An exchange

Finally leaving the hesitant shore,
driving to the house, carrying each other off
to bed, wishing you'd gone there sooner
instead of dawdling on the sand and in the shallows,
you find the beach has come with you
into the bedroom: here, too, rocks are underfoot,
seaweed continues to ripple between you,
light still curdles on a scrap of shell.
Give is the verb for you to conjugate,
inflecting voice, mood, tense, number, person.
And it's not that you give each other something.
Together you give yourselves
to the water, bit by bit.
You float, she twists and curls against your chest,
hands touch hips lightly. No need to be watchful:
you know your less than flawless bodies
are loosening, words coming free from the bone,
pieces of you slipping away
right out of sight.
Off with your crooked little toes,
the scars on skin or spirit,
your puny jokes and brittle explanations,
let them be off! – along with whatever
she wants to shed of herself.
Let them all go, props for Dada,
let them all sink deep into the sea,
the sea that gives you back yourselves
as you turn into each other, and ride
the strongest and gentlest of tides.

May

This afternoon is bringing
a long month to a standstill.

This afternoon is westering
to set afterthought at rest.

This afternoon is quaffing
goblets brimful of brandied light.

This afternoon is sloping
arms like shadows toward you.

This afternoon is hanging
hanging around
hanging around your neck.

Either way

Would you rather be defined
by agriculture or a gust of wind?
She was to either as you were to feathers
enveloped invisibly, just the other day,
passing the half-ploughed paddock.
She tugged you and filled you, as
over the furrow curve,
above the line unfurling brown from green,
a tractor towed a skinless balloon of seagulls.

Being drawn

Quickest to draw attention, she pulls
all particles of you into her pattern
like iron filings in a field of curves.
And that could be enough, except
that the lines arch only to and from herself.

Or you can take shape as if on paper:
she puts you right in the picture, puts you straight,
lifting the sag away from your shoulders.
But still the strong lines come from her hand alone.

Or, slowest of all, with care, she lifts you up
from a deep green well by the rope you once gave her.
She draws you out. You draw yourself up straight.

Coming to a sudden corner

Life's much too full
of what ifs and of might have beens,
forking paths or sliding doors,
to linger on regret
for anything unfinished;

yet I can't dispel
thoughts of that nanosecond when,
coming to a sudden corner,
I paused and turned
with longing undiminished

to glance behind, compel
my empty listless hand to wave,
but in the merest flickering
fraction of a moment
you had already vanished.

Growing like topsy, it goes like turvy

A letter arrives;
the weather slips into reverse.
Wind is tripping backwards, a leaf
flips up from grass to branch, turns
inside out, turns into a dowdy sparrow.
Again the hand picks up pages,
the eye picks out twists of phrase,
words winding widdershins,
the memory picks its way back
from end to beginning over a track
littered with assurances.
Love is a shadow sinking to the ground
as wind drops now into darkness.
Moths are starting to trickle up the window.
Frogs as glib as globular
swallow the night. In some throats
nothing sticks.

Restorative

Out of doors
there's still so much to mend
or to break in.
Bracken to clear, rain channels to dig,
grass to restore
where the builders left clay weals.
From the streaky window
everything looks askew.

Out of nowhere
a flamboyant robin comes
scalloping edges of the afternoon,
ties it with frills to a tea tree
that was hardly there before.
From time to time
from time, from time,
something like love takes shape.

Escapologists

Buried alive
they never panic.
Houdini's poise
is brittle beside theirs.
At last as if it's all
perfectly rehearsed
they break the surface
with uncanny timing,
primed for buds to burst.

Nor will you stay interred
in the heart's backyard.

Revenant

It was so clear that night
when drip by luminous drip
a lunar gleam like oil
slicked down the treetop
the shining seemed to give
a promise to hold tight
through thick and thin

but not so clear tonight
under this cloud-blackened sky
how or why the moon
that sank then through my eye
should surface now to stare
as we lie barely awake and light
is flaring on your skin.

Spring nuptials

First light cracks. Before the sun can touch
the upper surfaces, a ticking starts
in the green blood of hidden thin canals
as plaited fibres wake to creak and flex.
Networking messages are on the move
toward the airfront. Leaves get ready to lift
and face the great gold magnet. Let it roll!

The watchers feel bliss flutter, billow out –
a self-unfurling, sudden as the spill
of buds from branches on a time-lapse film.
Spring's things go bright with flagwag. Twigs perk up,
stretching akimbo. Seasonal semaphore
sends warm regards. This couple will turn over
leaves that are new enough to live forever.

Coming to our senses

1 Being heard

Before anything else happened,
before you had more than a hazy notion of how I looked
and long before we laid fingers on one other
or intimately knew our tastes and scents,
it was what we heard that opened us up –
not so much the words we spoke as their tone.
Some quality in your voice held a door ajar
and you told me later the timbre of mine
in that first tentative long-distance call
unlocked a chamber for you.
Perhaps I just sound
better on the phone, so should use it more
to converse with you, even when by your side?

2 Not looking too closely

We never wanted to see our life together
fixed and propped up in a shiny frame
or snapped into a stiff-leaf album
let alone shaped into Instagram grins
and these days we're even less keen
to have a lens pointed at us. When we come
across casual images of our former selves
they summon a kind of compassion because
we now know things that those more innocent
eyes and pliant bodies didn't yet know.

3 De gustibus

Taste isn't just about what tongues can feel
but also about what they utter. 'How sweet
are thy words unto my taste!' the psalmist said,
'Yea, sweeter than honey to my mouth.' Besides, he knew
that when it comes to the tang of sensory pleasure
mouth-feel has more allure than simple syrup.
For our part we've preferred the piquant flavours,
savouring remedies to anything that cloys,
relishing whatever smacks of the wry and dry.

4 Odoratissimum

To our mutual relief we soon discovered
that I didn't fancy an insistent perfume
any more than you'd like the whiff of aftershave.
Simple flesh, subtly redolent of everything
we give each other, has an ample fragrance.

5 Keeping in touch

Waking at night, we turn inquiringly
with sightless hands reaching each for each,
skin-checking that we're still here after all
this time.

Perching Ghosts

On your bike, Wordsworth!

Stripped of socks, shirt, and nearly of history,
you pedal along the top of the morning
towards the peninsula's tip:
sheer bodyhood purring on wheels.

This feeling, purely physical, simply present,
began to emerge last month
as the car curved through old valleys
out beyond Hahndorf
where 'the past' had shrunk to fragments, oddments
no longer fixed in time but whizzing towards you –
splat! on the mindscreen – like that tawny barn,
sunstruck, right out of nowhere, self-contained.
Then in the Coorong
windmill shadows tickled a salt lake pink
with reference to nothing bygone, and as you drove east
traces of earlier transits were few and thin:
sundry follicles of homeliness,
faint little leavings, taciturn chimneys.

Today you feel it more intensely still:
biking to Queenscliff
seems a way of shaking off all tales
of times you'd happened once upon.
Earlier journeys, deadlines, hardly impinge.
Even that cemetery of brassy helmets, near
the Point Lonsdale corner, demands no detour today.

It's your own corporal moment that seems to spill
into the countryside, your own bloodswoosh
that you hear in big-hearted pumpings of air
over hillocks while shrill spur-wings tick you off.
Who needs full recall now? Unlike the former
smoke of a hearth or scatter of ash,
your ectopulse erases grey chronometry –

ah, but then it strikes you: this beat that you're on
didn't begin with you! It's the ancient heartthrob
of interfusion, *I'm in the land and the land's in me,*
which brings back history, a shifty weight, as if
you've dinked a wobblesome Wordsworth along with you.
So puff goes presence of mind now he's on the scene,
gaunt phantom passenger, garrulous as ever,
proxy for any other old Father Time
who's littered the place with namings, notion-packed,
till none of it's fresh and you have no line of your own.

That's how it seems as you reach a mate's door at lunchtime.
Great day for beers and tucker, less great for chewing
the cud of each other's writing. It's hard enough
to follow your own composing rhythm, let alone
feel for the tempo
of someone else's lines; he hears a different drum,
the thump of limbs through bodies of water,
the stroke of a surfer, as you once thought of your feet
measuring the hills you ran beside. But now
you're poetry's pedaller,
shaping your metric with adroit machines
like landscape, as constructed as the wheel.

Time for the long push homeward, back on your bike,
with that senior ghost still perched on the handlebars.
And so you move past paddocks against the clock
while windy spokes go on singing to the cattle.

An earlier version of this poem appeared in the Festschrift *Mapped but not known*, in honour of Brian Elliott, who pioneered the academic study of Australian literature and became my PhD supervisor. His books include *The landscape of Australian poetry* and *Singing to the cattle,* both alluded to in my poem.

Elsewhere, elsewhen

The images swim their way through time,
awkward, willed, articulate,
inhabiting an incorrigible space,
filling absence like a cry…
– Paul Hetherington

A lash gets into your eye.
Sight is blurred as if by sticky memories
of strolling through and beyond the old
Botanic Gardens years ago. When the lid
is closed, the scratching's like a sharp
prickle of loss – a loss you never lose.
It's not a forgetting. Not a forfeiting.
After-images remain behind the lens
and you're no more distant now from any of them
than they were then from their own sources. Gaps
of absence were always felt. Every bizarre plant –
like all that the nearby gallery held,
and the museum, and university –
what they keep pointing to, so fugitive,
eluded you from the first. Even if you go
back there, you can't return to meanings
never fixed in place. Already in those days
as you mooched along the paths beside
old-world flowerbeds and deciduous trees
or scribbled your lecture notes or stared
at gilt-framed paintings and glassed-in specimens,
they were all representing *not* and *else,*
ambassadors of states far from your own.
The Gardens were a gazetteer
announcing foreignness, gulfs, distances.

Oak said England, baobab said Africa,
tokens of origin and possible destinations
but not of where you were, nor where you are.
Gallery conventions estranged the eye
and spoke of place exotically:
the cornering of paint poised in mid-air,
the bronze nipples of a statuette.
Museum items, too, were all far-fetched,
whether from shafts of space
(a chunky meteorite, scorched, pock-marked),
or from tracts of sea and snow
(weird whale ribs, a smooth-worn polar sledge),
or from quaint bygones
(Victorian costumery, old gold-toting coaches),
or from heroic shadows
(greenstone blades, great war canoes).
Across the road the university's
outlandish Gothic, like the far flung
reference frame for all its required reading,
was a further signpost to remoteness.
So simple? No. Those icons didn't merely
lead the tickled eye beyond local borders.
They enclosed within themselves
a sense of long deferral,

folding it into contours around that blank
centre of a huge *Dutch Funeral* canvas,
and of *Nor'wester in the Cemetery,*
and of the cave within the blue whale's bones
and of the elongated lawn behind
the clustered stone-pines, indecipherable
as photo blow-ups on a febrile screen,
and of the vacancy of Rutherford's room
in the quadrangle's crevice. What they all
said then, and go on saying now,
is neither *here* nor *there*.

In the foreground of this poem are various objects associated with a cluster of institutions in the New Zealand city where I lived for many years: the Christchurch Botanic Gardens, the Robert McDougall Art Gallery, the Canterbury Museum and the former city campus of the University of Canterbury.

Hanging on

The old retainers are surrounding you.
From oddment jars, leftover keys implore,
'Don't discard us yet! One of these days
we'll come in handy. So many things require
unlocking. In the long run you'll remember
where we fit, and why. Some happy hour,
with a smooth click, we'll turn for you again.'
Albums of photos clamour, 'Keep us here!
Each picture tells your story. We contain treasured
moments of your memory and desire.'
Rusty-hinged notebooks hoarded from schooldays,
yet never written in, say they need more
extended deadlines. Boxes of fading postcards
rattle for attention – listen! You can hear:
'Just hold us tight! We're full of messages
from misplaced friends.' Name tags recall each year
of conference-going. Worn-out copper coins,
scuffed shoes, wide ties, stretched cardigans, the flare
of trouser cuffs, packets of ancient seeds,
dried-up ink-bottles... You stare at the debris
then fling away the keys; what they might open
no longer holds a promise. Photos and cards
belonged to earlier selves; out with them now,
and out with all the other hoarded trash,
into the bin of past expiry dates
like rhymes that have lost their grip.
But the empty notebooks: those you'll keep.
They've waited blankly there for long enough,
and now you're ready to inscribe them all.

The Baths

They didn't call it a swimming pool back then.
Over the road from their school, it was just the Baths
where kids were sent to learn how not to drown –

a defensive knack, cheerless, devoid of hope.
To reach the school and the Baths beyond, he'd run
past the pussy willow at the foot of that steep slope

up a zigzag path to sycamores at the top,
grabbing winged seeds to pin as helicopters.
Malice could bring their playground games to a stop:

stabbed in the palm of his hand by a peevish brat
with a rusty screwdriver, he needed a tetanus shot,
and the sandpit castles built with his Chinese mate

got smashed each lunchtime by the Coleman set,
spitting words thick with spite about yellow skin.
Swimming lessons were even more drenched in threat.

Marched to the Baths, they changed into daggy togs
and stood in a huddle, thin arms wrapped over ribs,
a chill wind whipping their backs. Their twiggy legs

quivered. Water lapped. The long dank trough
glimmered with menace. Their teacher, Mr Brock,
walking behind each infant, gave them a shove.

The surface churned. They floundered, gasped, threshed, forced
their desperate way to the edge, clung there in shock.
So this was 'Learning To Swim' – and never to trust.

The Swamp

Itching to be big, the skinny kid
watched Vic's gang boot a footy to and fro.
At the paddock's edge, seepage was oozing through.

Someone kicked the ball near him. Chasing its bounce
towards the Swamp, he stumbled, sank at once
into the sticky green water-filth over his head.

If they hadn't dragged him out of the sucking mud
he would've drowned, they reckoned, drowned for sure.
Vic carried him home, sludge-stinky as a sewer.

Drowned! So deep-down dark, the sickening word
sounded as big as the Swamp. He shivered for hours
and was filled with slimy fearful shame for years.

Chums' Club

The glory and the freshness of a dream – William Wordsworth

There was a time when many a growing boy
would board a suburban bus on Saturday mornings
with ninepence in his pocket for admission
and under his arm a battered cardboard box
of cherished goods for barter.

Reaching Cathedral Square, he'd join a throng
that milled around the Crystal Palace foyer.
Of all the cheap cinemas in town, this one
was lowliest despite its grandiose name,
yet it had a special charter.

Chums' Club was more than movie time, although
celluloid tales beguiled with vision splendid
of men in masks: Zorro or Batman serials
brimful of menace, breathless with bravery –
and that was just for starters.

In the program's second half a feature film
had him agog. Adventure was the formula.
Cheering for Macdonald of the Mounties,
and when tall Tarzan met the Jungle Queen
sound effects from farters.

But the prime excitement came with Intermission:
time to negotiate swapping of comics. He learnt
the dialogues of business, the art of the deal.
Two Batman classics for *The Golden Helmet*? Done!
Next week he'd bargain smarter.

Chums' Club was a drumbeat for the dreams
of sub-adolescent boys in those noisy years
with heroes blazing on screens and pages, only
to fade into the light of common day
when time came for departure.

Wordsworth's 'Immortality Ode' was once an immensely popular
poem, its depiction of children as full of an innate brilliance that
fades as they become socialised being a constant point of cultural
reference throughout the Victorian period. Although the
Wordsworthian view of boyhood doesn't match my own recollection
of early experiences, I do remember affectionately something evoked
in his ode: the intensity of youthful imagination. So I've drawn here
on a few phrases from that poem, albeit in an ironic spirit. Chums'
Club did exist, but (as its unmodish name suggests) long ago,
though much closer to the present than to Wordsworth's time.

Bubblegumption

By the end of primary school we all fell sick
with shyness, straining to imagine what
to say to girls and how to get words out,
but we acted being game, rehearsing
a repertoire of casual gambits,
affecting a nonchalance so cool
it gave us the shivers.

Back then the art of conversation seldom
moved past the tip of a tremulous tongue
and insouciant smoking was beyond us
but having a dumb cud to chew with a studied
air of aplomb in lieu of spontaneous grace
gave our jaws an interim function that helped
to steady the jitters.

Though it was sickly sticky rubbery stuff
and we all knew better than to swallow it
we still needed something to screw
our courage to the sticking point
as words adhered to the mouth's roof
until at last they came out with a squawk
more awkward than ever

and the gist of whatever we blurted
was ignominiously empty, utterance
devoid of sense, let alone seduction –
as if a comic-book speech balloon
enclosed nothing at all, like a pink bubble
of utter vacuity that with a mortifying splat
blew up. Game over.

In over your head

You are the only two customers. Not until
the bartender is pouring your glass do you see
the other one has no arms, just stumps
that stop short where his elbows ought to be.
To drink he leans right forward, shoulders hunched
around the glass, and tips beer into his mouth.
Calling for a refill, he catches your eye
and speaks to you with a crackle of phlegm:
'Hey! Get the money for this from my pocket?'
You have to stand very close. His pocket is dirty,
and you can't find any money in it.
'Deeper!' he growls, chest rattling.
'Deeper!'

Small print

verso of a Berthing Slip, clause 14

*Subject to provision of Carriers Act, the Company
is not liable in respect of the passenger
for loss of life or for personal injury or illness
or in respect of goods for loss or damage
of whatsoever nature where the same
shall arise from or be occasioned by
the act of God, perils and accidents of the seas
or rivers, or machinery, boilers or steam navigation,
or other accidents, whether of a like nature
or otherwise,*

*or of default or error of judgement
or negligence of pilot master, mariners, engineers,
stevedores, servants or others employed by the Company,
whether in navigation or management of the steamers
or otherwise,*

*or of breach of warranty of steamers
or equipment, or of fire afloat or ashore,
delay or detention on the voyage, steamers not meeting,
compulsion by the Queen's enemies, Princes, Rulers or people,
quarantine, riots, strikes, lockouts, or other
labour disturbances, piracy, robbery or theft
by land or sea, whether by servants of the Company
or otherwise,*

or of effects of climate, heat of holds,
vermin on board, coaling on the voyage,
or for breakage of glass, china, earthenware,
cast-iron or other brittle or fragile goods
or for risk of craft or transshipment
or otherwise.

It all made me wonder how I ever survived
those multifarious potential mishaps,
wending my hazardous way from Wellington
to Lyttelton overnight (Cabin C238,
TEV Hinemoa), a passage so fraught
with such dire danger that my safe arrival
seemed quite miraculous: reaching the harbour
and shuffling down Gangway B totally unscathed
by any of those disasters, I felt like falling
to my grateful knees and kissing the quayside
but didn't because there was such a heavy frost
the smooch would have sealed my lips, and anyway
I needed to watch my footing on icy puddles,
a further menace unmentioned in clause 14
of the berthing slip, slipping twixt cup and lip,
and now I knew the world was rife with risks
too numerous to list, whether known unknowns
or otherwise.

Alfred Crusoe, apartment #8

Make the man-cave shine: that was his primary task,
brightening the sullen panels of one wall
and the dull blocky bricks of the others.
No sweat, accomplishing that transformation.
Radiant postcards here, radical posters there,
canary-yellow blanket on the bleak bed,
gaudy plastic to curtain off the shower,
fluorescent balloon afloat above the desk
as levity's flourish and a token of stretchy thought,
hung over a bottle, rakish, a scarlet hat –
in no time he felt quite luminous himself,
airily uplifted, sprightly as gossamer,
spring in his instep, tingle in his thumb-tip.

This lightness might have lasted, but for Duracell
longer-life batteries, the heavy duty sort,
solid, vital for his travel radio.
He began to ponder their hard-packed weight,
their tight electric muscle, pressed-down power
that draws force from the ground, earth current
darkly pulsing. *There* was a strength to build towards!
Instead of the lighter touch, the tighter grip!
He'd load up his body cells and living space
with gravity condensed! Searching for heaviness,
he came upon thick chunks of roadside rubble
and took them back to bench press till he ached,
kept bringing bigger rocks, power-lifting day
after day, watched biceps bulge and sinew swell,
found more and yet more massive slabs of stone,
crag fragments, dragged them hugger-mugger home,

covered the straining floor with might and main,
stacked them all tightly, row on compacted row,
higher, heftier, colossal, until last Friday
he could hardly squeeze out the door for a final load.

When he came staggering back, the apartment had gone
right through the floorboards, on through the earth's top crust,
leaving a hole like some huge stranger's footprint.

Zero

Ann Arbor, Michigan

They walk together on this icy path
and yet apart. Easy to guess that one
is older than the other: he stoops more,
bends knees more, sticks his elbows further out,
seems to expect to stumble. You can tell
that these are friends, though not quite at their ease;
that the older now is lonely, and the younger
soon will be lonely too; that neither will
admit such frailties. Their thick boots creak
and slither. Both men laugh, one at a time.

Later, from a doorway, the younger one
looks out at somebody's future: there he sees
a leaf-blade scrape across a frozen skin,
then beyond that a huddle of thin trees
and further back a last shiver of sun.

He watches his tired friend shovel the snow.
The weather forecast is for deepening cold.

Evening out

Here the great western leveller unfolds
on every side a dream of blackened fields.
No sea's horizon
could be more even.

Love in the afternoon will peel it all
back, as if this plain were just a roll
of turf – or a blanket
tossed by an ankle.

Below? At first you'd think what's underneath
is party time: ants on the tablecloth,
bright bubbles drifting
to burst with laughter.

But blood and bone lie deeper. Darkness pulls
over your head a layer that recalls
an evening margin
of the oldest ocean.

Walhalla

You're standing on a tilted slab of stone
when *Whoosh!* Out spins a speedy bird that must
have made its nest inside the hollow grave.

Birds aren't too fussy. It's a place to live.
No worries here about the trace of dust.
Easy to share the space with a packet of bone –

if you're a bird. On the shadow side, recessed,
there's a small door, shut tight. The handle's gone.
A keyhole's left, but the key is lost.

Finally

Take your future for a walk
past stone-wrapped residues of lives.

Pick your way along the rows
of epitaphs, all that survives

to tell us who these remnants were
or what they meant to anyone.

Block after block of memories
bleached bone-white by a blazing sun

show how stony the years can be,
how pitiless, how unforgiving.

Fragments buried here knew once
what it felt like to be living,

Reprieved

Take your future for a walk
round Alfred Cove. The big birds glide

convergingly, and wind fills out
spinnakers on the Claremont side.

Dolphins turn like serrated wheels.
'Every result is clear.' Such grins

all over those pelican faces!
Sentence ends. The next begins.

Cured

After cutting off his head
she felt much better. Decapitation
rendered the naked body
nicely anonymous.
Just a male trunk and limbs now,
mere flesh without identity.

For a long while she stared
at the headless torso,
the strongly muscled arms and legs.
His physique had impressed her once.
Pleased with it himself, he liked
to pose nude for her camera.

She used to savour his saltiness:
his coarse tongue, his sweaty body.
'Trim, eh?' he'd say with a wink,
fondly patting his chest. Now
it was different. Trimmed.
A truncation well deserved.

Taking an envelope from her desk,
she wrote in bold block capitals
his name, his address. Then,
slipping the snipped photo inside,
she licked the tangy flap and sealed
the surprise, ready for posting.

Blank desertion

Wharram Percy, Yorkshire

Green banks deepen. Doubtful, your path tilts down
slowly below the gusts, below your time,
below the level of a tractor ploughing.
Thorn bushes line the sunken passage. Then
you reach an open field, a wind more chill,
a bridge across a stream, a rowan grove,
and this old pressure: wordless, heavy, dark.

Beyond, the path goes on – to emptiness.
You see the imprint of the long-gone homes
there in the grass like floor plans roughly sketched.
Further on still, the relic of a church:
some walls are standing. Each wind's eye is narrowed.
Nothing can keep out the trenchant cold.

The strangeness of it! – not in what you've found
but in the act of coming here: that long
uncertain path descending from one age
into another. Back you climb, to where
the tractor ploughs the same strip as before.

The title phrase comes from the boat-stealing passage in Book 1 of Wordsworth's autobiographical poem 'The Prelude'.

A goose, too, is a bird of poetry

Ithaca, New York

Abruptly the year turns down a notch,
changes gear, direction.
Uneasy time to arrive, leaves
flustering skittish chipmunks on the lawn.
Season of fidgets
or of bold new bearings?
So soon after hoisting yourself northwards
it's disconcerting to see overhead
these geese rush whooping to the south.
Migration for them is fully projective, it means
sticking the neck right out, jointly alive
as they fly with companionable accord,
one line that ripples, macro-wave,
wings of a single bird.

The title responds indirectly to Robert Duncan's poem 'An owl is an only bird of poetry.' Duncan's early work was associated with the Black Mountain School's 'projective verse' – alluded to in my description of the way in which geese fly. At the time, I was co-editing the book *Robert Duncan: scales of the marvellous* for the American publisher New Directions.

Dogged by Sirius

Belgrade Lakes, Maine

A grand occasion, it was to have been: tonight
after so long standing on his head
Orion at last would swing himself upright
above these watchful waters.
No such luck. Turns out he's out of season
in this hemisphere. The hefty huntsman
took his slow dive down through the horizon
just days ago into that nether space
where the head still hangs below the belt.
But his dog is lingering hereabouts
and under cover of darkness
gives the lake a licking.

Next morning, family photos from the jetty
and everything looks tranquil
to the camera. Sun-spread is candid,
leaves are gleaming. This pond might seem
to mirror an absolute promise
except for the sneaky bloodhound
continuing to lurk unseen.

The game is venery. The heart is a lonely
haunted lake, its lifeblood lapped by regret.
Time now to sink deep into the water.
On Orion's trail you have to take the plunge,
going under before you can come up.

A traction

Chinon, Vale de Loire

Intending to stop for an hour, you stay for days.
So narrow, this place, so long drawn out, you can't
get to the end of it
down that warped tunnel of centuries.

This is one of the spots where
Rabelais swapped flat bread for round phrases.
This is one of the spots where
Joan the Maid unmanned the unmannerly.
This is one of the spots where
Richard the Lionheart died.

Splendour stalls at the château walls.
On its lawns a peacock, all eyes,
has no regard for Richelieu, Eleanor, Agnès.
This is one of the spots where
time takes you lightly.

Reclamation

Chek Lap Kok airport, Hong Kong, 1998

How to enlarge an island: cut it down
to size. Then level it off, spread packed debris
further into the water, forming a field
of rubble thick enough to bear the weight
of anything the outside world will fly in.

A new airport – and something more? The region
itself, reclaimed: will it be flattened out?
Social compaction, wheel upon common weal?
Those crusher machines, slowly pushing the soil
back and down beneath them, look like tanks.

The future is preparing to descend.

Breathless

Nuclear-powered vessels acquired through AUKUS will ensure that submariners can stay underwater for a very long time. A Defence Department source describes this as a 'breathtaking advance' in operational capability. (News report)

Tomorrow we'll be going our separate ways.
For you it's the long deep-down immersive journey
to inaugurate your careers, taking the plunge
while I wheeze into retirement with a bronchial curse.
This being my last address to departing recruits,
it's time to discard the usual formula. So
no ponderous jokes, no patriotic clichés,
no orthodox advice. Instead, here's just

a frankly unpleasant message before your first
grand voyage begins. I won't tiptoe around it:
you ought to picture what may lie in wait –
and if it's too much to stomach, don't proceed!
That isn't cowardice. It's about imagining.
Better to pull out now and stay on shore
than have a panic attack miles underwater
that could spell utter havoc for you all.

Although the risk of disaster is fairly small
it's no remote abstraction. You've probably seen
those news reports in recent months. Wartime
wreckage on the ocean floor. Lost subs.
Envisage that. Let your mind dwell on the scene
and on how those sardines died, gasping their last.
For any submariner this is never far away,
stark fear of suffocation. No defence:

as soon as a vessel's hull is breached, intense
water pressure will cause your lungs to collapse.
Nitrogen, more soluble than oxygen,
will dissolve and fill your blood, causing
asphyxiation from the inside out.
Now let me guess: you're thinking 'Well, at least
it will all be over quickly. A rush, a crush
and splat! I'm gone.' But not so fast, my friends!

Consider an alternative: the drawn-out end
of HMS *P-311* off the Sardinian coast,
where it has lain since 1942
with 71 bodies still enclosed.
Only the prow shows any damage.
Its inner chamber seems to be intact
so it must have sunk with air sealed tight inside,
and the crew died slowly, feeling their oxygen wane.

One final thing. If you do opt to remain
on shore when your boat leaves port, remember this:
there's no assurance you'll go on breathing
by staying on terra firma. Most of us
will suffocate at the end, lungs overwhelmed,
as if sucked back to where living once began,
submerged in the sea, before anyone ever inhaled.
Don't like the thought? Then how do you see your last phase?

For obvious reasons, submariners are known as 'sardines.' The island of Sardinia derived its name from the small oily fish that were once abundant in the sea around it. Off the coast there, the wreck of HMS *P-331* was found sixty-four years after it sank, newly commissioned and before the conferral of its intended name – *Tutankhamun*. It remains on the sea floor, a largely intact coffin.

Filial Shadows

So long

1 The stoop

Things that hook their talons in memory's gut
after deep-diving down a shaft of years
are not like a standard relic or mere leftover

such as his musty coat, his yellowing silk scarf,
those books all foxed and boxed, the dry fountain pen,
his fading letters in a hand as firm as ever.

Reminders are random now, like this one,
startling, obliquely barbed: away up there
on a high roof ridge, scanning the marble river,

an osprey crouches. Its white-hooded head
could be a cowl – an executioner's
or even a victim's. Raptors know how to sever

a lifeline suddenly, plummeting to snatch
the quarry hidden under a samite surface,
slice it apart and savour every sliver.

2 The unknowing

As far as I know
my father doesn't know
that he's long dead.

Though his deadness now
is the main thing known about him,
these days only a few are left who know it.

I do. My sisters do. That's about it.
After so long, others who used to know
have – or have been – forgotten.

His death was quick
as the stoop of an osprey
but his deadness goes on, long and slow,

travelling with me farther along the track
towards my own unknowing.
So long, Dad, so long.

Chip to old block

On the sloping paddocks where you grew up
this thick grey lump could be mistaken
at first glance for a weathered cowpat
but it's a chunky sawn-off wooden stump,

crevice-cheeked, shadow-smeared.
Crumbs of soil that seem to drop
from its ridges and deep furrows
hint at falling flakes of ash.

Fearing your final face might look
collapsed and battered like this block,
I refused to 'view' your corpse –
a craven error. I was young.

Instead, since then, I've searched for you
in oddments left behind: letters, clothes,
keepsakes, photos, spiritless things,
none of which could tell me much.

And so, old block, I'll try to summon
semblances of what you may have been
by dropping a few lines to you and hoping
to glimpse you somewhere in between.

The coat

After years in a storage suitcase
it gets its first post-mortem airing:
my father's gabardine coat, one of the relics
given me when he died. Shoving my fists
deep in the pockets, I touch shreds of tobacco.

For forty years he rolled his own. Always
he would be smoking. And that day when his heart
gave its last cough, they found him slumped at his desk
with a bent cigarette beside his face.
Later I saw him disappear
through curtains of the crematorium
to go on smoking.

I have my hands in his pockets
and in my hands his brittle remains.

Ticker

That was his nickname among friends and siblings.
Explanations differed, his own bland version being
that each coat peg outside his infant classroom
had carried its distinctive identifying image
to help kids mystified by written words
and the one assigned to him
depicted a clock.

That fits. I think of the way he later tended
our clunky mantelpiece Ansonia
winding it up last thing each evening
and keeping it precisely five minutes fast
so its hourly strike would prime us for radio news
not drown it out.

Ah no, said one his sisters, he was Ticker because
he always used to chatter incessantly
like a two-bob watch.

Whatever its origin, I like to think the moniker
was apt for a man who had a big soft heart
and could readily chat about anything
except deep feelings.

And just as his children approached the age
when he might have begun to talk with us
about those murky difficult vital things
it was his ticker that failed and felled him
without a warning, so we never quite discovered
what made him tick.

On the wharf

My eyes are lowered as if looking for something
lost a long while back.
But I've never come down this path before.
Must have to do
with being near a waterfront like this
near other sudden hills.
Can't work out where –
until, as if sleepwalking, I step up
and tread with smaller feet along the low
top of a shady wall.
And then I know
I'm back in Wellington, I'm five years old,
wanting my dad to lift me on his shoulder.

Too late for that. Perhaps there's time to send
a postcard to my children, signed *Anchises*.

The closing lines allude to Book 2 of Virgil's *Aeneid*, where the eponymous hero carries his father Anchises out of the flames of Troy.

The company of milk

Each morning, music would rise up to the office
of the dairy superintendent: he'd hear the usual
sing-song of churns trundled over wet concrete
for loading onto the trays of lined-up trucks
and a higher note too, the ping of water
jetting from hoses against the huge steel vats.

Proud of his role in 'the second-biggest
milk company in the southern hemisphere',
managing the whole process, he liked to recall
where this work began for him: the milking shed
on his family's Hawera farm, and then hard years
of yakka in a cheese factory down the road.

Yet the calling may have come from further back,
beyond his conscious memory, the merest
dreamlike trace of a lingering sensation:
the primal bodily comfort of an infant
nestled calmly against a soft warm breast
and sipping the creamy juice of nourishment.

A pencilled message

He was once a wielder of fountain pens
who rested his papers on a large blotting pad
as he wrote, turning them often on their face
so the signature flourish (oddly resembling mine)
would be protected from smudges, and in the process
leave its ghostly image there in reverse.

But now, a spectre himself, still at that small desk,
he's become a thin pencilled message
whose fading imprint gets fainter with each
forgetful year. Partly erased, he is hardly
decipherable except when someone may call him
to mind and to paper, bringing his hand within reach.

Our Pelorus

Pelorus: a non-directive navigational device for maintaining the relative bearing of a vessel at sea

Pelorus Bridge, Pelorus Sound, Pelorus Jack:
story-crammed names that in our childhood
charmed us with the power of amulets.

'Tell us again about the famous dolphin.'
'Well, he guided Cook Strait sailors safely back
year after year. That was Pelorus Jack –
only creature in the world, they say,
protected by a parliamentary act –
he was a wonder. Smarter than human pilots.'

'And what about the time when that big earthquake
shook Pelorus Bridge while you were at school?'
'Oh, you've heard all that.' 'Tell us again!' So she did.
Our mother had a stock of other tales as well
about her natal district: fires, floods, felling
and milling of rimu, swimming in the river,
picnic excursions to Pelorus Sound.

We didn't know then that those Peloruses
referenced the first ship to explore the Sound,
nor that in turn the British sloop's own label
came from an instrument which itself was named
for Hannibal's pilot. Thanks, etymology!

But we did know this: the cryptic word was bound
tightly with our mum's power, when we were all at sea,
to guide our bearings and stop us running aground.

Foxhill

Share the rest out between husbands
but scatter some of her ashes here
where her great-grandparents have waited
in a silence that slopes into shaky darkness
between Wakefield and the Murchison range.

She loved this place, and it will absorb her now.
Not a fox or a foxglove to be seen, just deer
and cattle politely tending the paddocks.
Also, inevitably, sheep, less decorous.

Still the dark macrocarpas keep you serious.
Sunlight subsides. Gravestones forget their lines.
Too late to get your caravan on the road,
so pause and spend
a last night here with her, mother and friend.

Catching up

Incongruously vapid, yet it's a phrase that loiters
beside an image of my long-absent mother
as I watch the gap between the age I'm at
and the standpoint where she remains
rapidly shrink.

She seems immobile there, while distance looks
in my direction. She waits for me to catch up,
though not expectantly. Steadfast, as always,
and patient as a weather-worn statue or
stolid tombstone.

Won't be long now until I reach her station.
When I arrive it will be a kind of catch-up
but one that won't allow us to sit and chat
about our inexorable convergence or
anything else.

What's in a name?

So much depends
upon
a well-reared
bearer
of lineage and
a name.

Consider my 3 times great
paternal grandfather who
whispered history has it
was an amateur Irish Romeo
under cover of the ludicrous moniker
Clotworthy.

Try that again on your tittering tongue
A pleasure to meet you
I'm Clotworthy.

Hardly a charming tag to conjure with
you'd think
even in County Antrim.

Yet a venturesome chatterbox
could turn embarrassment
to sly advantage.

My name's not the uttermost
extent to which I'm singular
as you can soon discover
if you let me be a lingerer
around your life, Miss Blane.

Coagulation
here he'd lift a suggestive eyebrow archly
is just one of my specialties.

And so they came together
and so
long after his blather
had wrought its merry magic
a bloodline meandered erratically
through all the intricate vessels
of successive generations
heart to heart along such tenuous
pathways where each quick throb
no matter how erotic
could be so easily blocked
that any of us at any time
might well become thrombotic
in everything but name.

Matrimonial trigonometry

Their marriage was as three-sided
as County Antrim itself.
The place that cornered their spirit
surely belonged to Ireland
but still was ruled by England
and settled by Ulster Scots.
No wonder they felt as divided

as the most unholy
trinity, three-in-two.
Always a third party
intersected this pair:
he and she plus the man
he might have been or might
yet hope to be – solely

single but triply double,
a couple of souls rendered
triadic by having wed
a ghost in the mind's mirror,
a hopeful hypotenuse
that became a slippery slope
down into mundane trouble.

Restricted entry

Brassy, small, worn smooth, lower down
than handles on any ordinary doors,
this loose knob sags with years of sheer fatigue
and rattles, taking a while to grip the catch.
Red paint gleams on its narrow-board surface,
latest of thick-daubed coats to fill the grooves
of weathering history; no trace of grain.
The threshold plank is registrar of boots
and platform for the cheekiest of chooks.
Behind the door, a glimpse of your boyhood
and beyond that, a dim ancestral past.

If you were to arrive at the old farm,
knock knock, Aunt Lorna would appear, squinting,
squeak her 'Good Heavens,' tell you that you look
'*just* the way poor old Ticker used to look,'
and then, putting the chuckling kettle on,
she'd dig out photo albums ('Chip off the block!').
The panelled walls would look the same, and hear
the same old jokes ('Those borer must hold hands!').
Furniture, all made by Grandpa's own
lump-knuckled hands, would be unchanged since when
school holidays were spent there, playing chores.

Later you'd go out that other door
past all the tiny scarlet money spiders
sprinting madly over blotchy concrete
near the front steps, and glance towards the shed
where your Dad, they say, studied after each day's
stint at the cheese factory, and Uncle George
squeezed out the bagpipes; on past the boxthorn hedge,
and past that garage, cut into the hill,
which used to shelter the old Lexington
with its oval perspex window at the back,
down the soft slope to the green-orange-white
lichen-patched bridge across the weedy swamp,
and over to the marvellous milking shed
with its long cold hard pump handle and its wide
carpet of cowpats, and from there you'd look
across the upper paddocks, shadow-barred,
to the dented peak of Egmont, and look down
the hill to the other side, where the rails run
to carry skim milk on a trolley, which you'd ride too,
zoom past the mightiest cabbages in the land,
to pigsty squelch and a whole new world of smells.

You wouldn't go around the hidden dark
side of the house, along the forbidden path
that leads to the grim slaughterhouse. You did
creep up there once, many decades ago,
inquisitive, timid, knowing Grandpa
had just gone in with a cleaver. As you peered
around the doorway, his bent figure turned,
gripping the blade, and with an air of menace
began to sharpen it noisily on a steel,
and then hissed a dreadful question: 'Anyone
see you come in, little boy?' You fled in panic,
pursued by your own shrieks and his guffaws.

Longingly in longhand

Filed in old folders
tossed in a bottom drawer
or tucked into the pages of a book
they summon up times past – not only
because most were inscribed long years ago
and some by hands untouchable now
but also because few of us ever
send such personal things
in longhand any longer.

Boldly rounded
or dainty-spindly upright
or toppling forward or leaning back
their calligraphy seemed to mimic attributes
of the one who held the pen. But regardless of tone
or motive, the form itself inherently implied
that the mere act of writing letters
by hand was wistfully offering
intimacy even to a stranger.

Like the V-flap
of an envelope licked
by tongue and sealed by finger
the message contained inside was also
whatever its particular purpose or inflection
a container in its turn, enclosing within it
an intangible gift that whispered
Inside my words is a longing
that continues to linger.

Thrifty optimism

Dead now, most of them, but I remember yet
a frugal generation, habits formed
through onerous years of hardship, scrimping, fret.

They'd save bent nails or rusty screws in old
tobacco tins with sundry odds and ends
like bow-tied bits of string, trying to hold

fast to a faith that things would come in handy
some rainy day, to vindicate their prudence.
'Fashion' meant nothing. They'd look askance at 'trendy.'

Used clothes and other hand-me-downs were all
as precious as old-time songs, as well-worn rings.
Dad's tartan tie, or Grandma's favourite shawl,

or Aunty Nell's big brooch, were gifts to treasure
like clippings stuck in scrapbooks, souvenirs,
or motley keepsakes cherished beyond measure.

Repurposed wool could knit a life together
when something had unravelled. A stitch in time
could save the whole darned family in foul weather.

They were conservators. Each hoarded scrap
honoured ideals of continuity.
Thrift didn't stem from fear of a poverty trap;

it wasn't about being short of cash; above
all such concerns, they simply longed to clasp
a residual hope in things others had loved.

All thumbs

The cleverest human features
come in pairs
like eyes and ears
like testicles and breasts
and so too with opposable digits
supposed to be the most
definitive trick of our species
a smart device that assists
fine motor skills and brings
precision to our fidgets.

You've taken it all for granted
over the years
when time has been neatly jointed
but as each hinge
at the base of those paired phalanges
starts to go numb and then
succumbs to acute arthritis
the sight of a screw-top jar
or a weedy patch of garden
fills you with winces and cringes.

Now you're watching your grandkids
clutch screen gadgetry
for rapid messages –
and it seems the process of digital
evolution still persists:
to hold pen to paper with fingers
is for them a strenuous endeavour
yet instead their cohort becomes
the first generation ever
to write with both of their thumbs.

Ageing

on a beach at dusk
you watch the shallows ripple
where tomorrow drifts

*

after the big storm
this grey she-oak standing tall
ignores you again

*

old toes curl sideways
veering away to avoid
that big step ahead

*

inhaling deeply
any long breath sweet or sour
as if it's the last

*

click-clock on the wall
hasn't learnt to tell the time
remaining for you

Speaking Pictures

Simmo's aphorism

Simonides of Keos said that poems
were speaking pictures, pictures silent poems.
Up to a point, Simmo, up to a point.

Pictures are just for eyes; poems for eyes
but also for ears. So now let's dot our i's:
poems may sing, Simmo, sing to the paint.

Pictures can only cast a wordless look
at poems, yet poems can tell how pictures look
or what they bring to mind, without constraint.

But OK, Simmo, no doubt you'd protest
that you know this, that Plutarch failed the test
of accurate translation. Fair complaint.

The Romans oversimplified, we know,
their borrowings from Greeks. For all we know
there was more subtlety in your viewpoint.

Let's assume so, agreeing on this point:
when they give pictures a fresh lick of paint,
poems do the talking, and dance the talk – en pointe.

Never satisfied with seeing

after a painting by Jill Kempson, *The olive grove*

At first glance, almost Arcadian: the last
languorous phase of afternoon has lingered
in this quiet orchard. Yet, lowering above
the backlit trees, clouds thicken. Dark bands reach
across the glimmer of the middle distance.
Not so idyllic, then. What makes it seem
suffused with eeriness? Is it the way
puffed-up foliage mimics those nimbus shrouds
masking the horizon? Something in the fall
of light that brings the stealthy shadows
creeping closer? A hint of gusts, as 'wind
returns again according to its circuits'?
Absence of people? Murkiness drifting near,
choking that last faint sunglow? 'The eye is never
satisfied with seeing,' said the Preacher.
Imagining can spook us. Let's get out of here.

The quoted phrases come from the King James translation of the Old Testament book of 'Ecclesiastes, or the Preacher', chapter 1. Patrick Le Chanu cites verses 5 to 8 of this chapter as an epigraph to his book *Jill Kempson's Oeuvre: Landscape in Perspective*.

Watering the land

after a pair of landscape paintings by Jennifer Hopewell

Miraculous, this transforming paradox
intrinsic to the medium itself:

dry particles of pigment are dissolved
by water that holds them briefly in suspension

and then performs a strange alchemical act
as patches of brushed colour form

layers that interplay, patterns that verge
on sheer abstraction while at the same time

starkly depicting tracts of rock and scrub
in an arid landscape we'd thought we knew until

water brought this bright change, no longer seen
as through a glass darkly, but now face to place.

Vital signs

after a painting by Judy Cassab, *Still life with blue table*

There's always a sly irony
at this genre's heart:
life, in fact, can seldom
be stilled for long, so
objects artfully arranged
will soon begin to move again
unless they've expired.

Cassab's picture draws
the eye only to tease it,
thwarting interpretation.
It gestures toward the real
in an oddly angled way
as if to make us fish
for a catch of meaning.

More of a clutter
than a neat composition,
objects on the blue table
may seem moribund.
This twiggy plant
is turning into a trident
while that cylinder

looks like a pot, but
a pot of what? The bottle
is nearly necrotic
and is that a mirror
reflecting death's door?
Surfaces appear to lie
on tilted planes.

Yet after all
it's not in the least inert.
The paintwork is full
of intense uneasiness –
a vital sign –
alive precisely because
it won't stay still.

Hanging in the Discharge Lounge

after a painting by Henri Matisse, *The open window, Collioure*

Flesh-pink French doors opening
inwards to where we stand
draw our gaze outwards
past a quadrille of small craft
that gesture brightly at the hazy bay
in a semaphore of departure

as if an incisive scalpel
had peeled back delicately
two vivid flaps of skin
to reveal a balcony framed
by swirls of sturdy plants
and beyond them the lucent water

so that all of it suddenly discloses
the subtle operations of a world
where insight and outlook converge
and manage to transfer to us
the knack of looking both ways at once
from our vantage between past and future.

Silk on cinnabar

after a painting by Ben Joel, *The great seal*

Withstanding years of earnest scrutiny,
this painting remains tight-lipped, gives little away.
But its title conjures a world where Kublai Khan

presents to Marco Polo a tablet of gold
imprinted with his great seal and inscribed
with a message vouching for its intrepid envoy.

The seal's ink paste itself, Marco records,
is made of cinnabar, mulberry-red
– much the same colour as this picture's ground.

Thin oblong figures, strands of creamy silk
arranged in rows, box-like, appear to float
on the painted surface, indecipherable.

In the murk behind them there are hints
of limbs that sprawl, as if a body is either
idly receptive or almost falling apart.

Beneath the patterning, something unruly stirs.
Nearly discernible, is that your phantom self
emerging from shadows of a fabled past?

Somnambulist

after a collage by Mikaela Castledine, *Sleepwalking*

Immensity surrounds the puny figure:
a spangled night sky, huge, yawning above
the mighty lake that stretches out beside him.
Who would venture there alone – exposed,
squeezed between vast expanses – except in dreams?
What on earth is he thinking? Is he an outback
Pascal, or semi-Rousseau, a solitary
promeneur, darkling, sunk in reveries,
stranded in eternal silence, terrified
by these infinite spaces? Or does he feel calmly at home
in his private cosmos, comfortable creature of stars?
Wandering back to our camp, he has nothing to tell us.
A deeply secretive dreamer, he keeps his own
sleepy counsel. But if we could know his mind
we might well discover that it mirrors ours –
that we're all steeped in somnolence, ambling along
through endless darkness, unable ever to wake.

Stony silence

after a painting by Mary Knott, *Rough cast in stone*

A village in some Umbria of the mind:
that's where the church tower seems to belong,
and those terracotta roofs, those roughcast walls.
But this is no postcard cliché. The many small
windows, deep-set, dark, have an eyeless look
as if from too much gazing, sight withdrawn
into a fearful blindness of empty sockets.

What did they see that blackened their vision?
More than the glare of sunlight striking stone?
Is anybody home to answer these questions?
Is the whole place abandoned? How long since
its belltower uttered a sound? Who can say?
Silent and sightless, incommunicado,
windows and walls have nothing to report.

Yet this picture's far from taciturn. It hints
that the buildings are weaker than the foreground shapes
which in time will tame what they now confront.
Shoulder to shoulder stand the sombre trees,
prepared to show no mercy. Oh, it's not
for nothing that they're called stone pines. They stare
unblinking, and are hardening their hearts.

Incident on table 4

after an etching by Holley Chirot, *Death at Schrafft's*

Her lolling body will need to be removed
without putting people off their food. Meanwhile
this gesture of discretion must suffice:
a screen around the inconvenient table
like a bracket closing off her life.

It gets to you, though. Head waiter's quite upset
and I'm seeing our décor in a darker light.
The chequered flooring makes me think of chess –
that line from Omar Khayyam. Those pillars, too:
their elephantine toenails, quite bizarre,
remind me of what I read somewhere
about how the giant creatures seem to mourn
when a fellow pachyderm dies, shuffling around
the corpse and nudging it with careful feet
in measures of grief.

Can someone dim the globe in that lamp overhead?
It used to look vividly floral; now it's garish.
Lighting should reflect the fact that she's dead
is bad for business, worse for her. No place to perish!

A hooded boat

after a painting by Rick Amor, *Out to sea*

The watcher has walked through the frowning light of dawn
to scan this weather, scowl at swollen clouds,
see his friend's boat push out against the current.

When it moves past him towards open water
he'll be unnerved, glimpsing a gothic figure
under that shadowy cowl – as if some foreboding,
face to face with his friend, has blackened the skiff.

Then his eye will follow the thick line of a wall
along to the tall pale building. From beneath
a steepled brow, it has seen many another
set out to sea, dark-hooded, and some come back.

Come back! Come back! A dirge whines in the wind.
This boat isn't only his friend's. Here the watcher sees
a crouching spectral self, his own funereal emblem.

Amphibious

after an etching by John Olsen, *The escape*

What is he rushing away from, the scrawny frog?
A French kitchen knife? Unlikely. Those lean thighs
lack the succulence that first attracted
medieval monks, hungry for flesh but forbidden
to eat any meat, who devised a tasty dish
by simply classifying frogs as fish.
Some other predator, then, perhaps a bird
which (his grin shows) he's managed to elude.

Or is there no menace? Nothing behind him to fear?
If there's a safe zone, perhaps he's in it already,
an imaginary stretch of beach between the flags,
shielded by lilypads like elevated parasols.
The sense of release may be its own reward,
a luxurious end in itself, merely the sheer
bliss of skinny-dip swimming, especially as it's not
your classic froggy breaststroke: this guy's arm
is lifted at the elbow, his webby digits
pulling him freestyle through the water, while
a turbo flutter-kick propels him forward.
It's the true Australian crawl, streamlined and speedy,
apt for enrapt amphibians – our great escape.

Not so black and white

after a digital image by Matthew King, *Dark figures*

At first glance it's the birds
that dominate in all their
chanceless unpredictability
as a flurry of backlit wings
lifts your sight skywards
almost filling the frame
with sheer flightiness

but then a sombre human
silhouette looms up
out of the corner of your eye
like a shadow of lurking guilt

so you're nearly convinced
to see in this whole array
a parable of shimmery light
always flirting with all that's dark

and yet there's more going on
than mere chiaroscuro. Look how
the pale blue tinted edge of the bollard
picks up those distant lines
that hint at a wash of water
taking you back to the blankness of paper
where the play of colour is never far away.

Dead, naked in the looking glass

Double exposure sticks two pictures together.
One is of Mallarmé: afraid he might vanish
into thin air behind his own back, he'd often
do his writing in front of a mirror
to keep a keen eye on himself.
Ideally he would have liked to go
right through the looking glass,
stay on that other side where no sun's ray
could strike his skin, nor any clock
snicker as thin hands move over paper.
Only there could he remove his clothes.

Imprinted over that, an old dream fragment
that kept turning slowly through you, long after
you once almost slithered into a crevasse:
the dream of a bare nacreous arm
being squeezed out through the split
face of a glacier.

The title refers to a line in Stéphane Mallarmé's 'Sonnet en X'. My dream of a corpse preserved in ice may have come from an incident half a century ago when a teenager was caught by an avalanche in New Zealand's Southern Alps (near where I once had a mountaineering accident myself) and his body was not found – until forty-two years later, when it appeared at the edge of the Tasman Glacier.

Other Bodies

Sea-changes

On the far side of your mask each animal
and mineral has gone all vege-troppo:
Atlantis floribunda! Architects
cluster on roofs down there, make crusty plans
for plant-like penthouses, extension cells.
You're sixty miles from land, but traffic flares
beneath you, flowers with natty fins drift past
apartment blocks and stalk small movers down.

Hoisting your sea-legs up the pontoon steps,
you turn to watch her flotage: there she goes!
a submarine hang glider out beyond
that ledge of coral,
sudden blueness steepening below.

Civvies again; decked out for promenade,
this lubber underrates a wayward breeze.
Swish! And your debonair prop spins overboard.
Rescued by boathook, the draggled panama
Will never look the same. On the high seas
of the voyage back, the boat splat-whumps along
while every gorge goes giddy, and your own
spontaneously overflows and overflows.
The wharf returns after a thousand hours.

Hotel. Into your longest ever shower –
still fully clothed. No pocket left unturned,
no trace of the belly's mutiny unrinsed,
you pat your wobbles dry, and so to bed.

Later, attempting convalescence, you lie
feebly underneath the palm-trees, feel
the light recede like ebbing of the blood,
and vow never to leave your element.
Yet some seem easily amphibious:
above the fronds, shouldering hidden currents,
a black kite slides a slow curl down its wing
like a trim-cut airborne stingray.
Thanks, you think. But you'll walk.

Be careful what you fish for

A few moments ago
this river was entirely still
and the air above it just as calm
but then from behind me a raptor
rushed past my shoulder
and on down below me in a flash
to rupture the water
sending the surface into a dazzle of splinters

only to struggle as its take-off turned
into a frantic flurry of thrash and splash
weighed down by water on its wings
and the flapping of a large flathead
clamped in its talons –
too heavy a choice this time
the osprey must have thought –
until at last it somehow managed
to labour upwards
while the big fish kept on wriggling
though lighter now than before being seized
because its heedless neatly severed head
had sunk beneath the surface.

Out of place

1 A trespass

Entering your bedroom, you click on the light
and something rattles. A little earthquake?
No. Everything's quiet and still except
for one small noise over on that far wall
where a large painting seems all aquiver.
Tentative, you peek behind the vibrating frame.
A micro bat, wings mantling its eyes,
crouches there, tremulous, in disguise
as a miniature collapsed pup tent.

No caped crusader this, nor snaggletooth vampire
nor vengeful *Fledermaus*. Just a local denizen,
bashfully reclusive most of the time,
and in this case an accidental trespasser
who, in hot pursuit of a moth, sped through
your doorway inadvertently, and then,
feeling the need for a quick nap,
sneaked beneath the picture, only for a slap
of brightness to tweak it rudely awake.

Yet if a trespass has occurred,
might it not be your own?
To the zippy bat, intent on a hunt that enacts
multi-millennial habits of its kin,
your property is merely an irksome
intrusion on unceded airspace, a stricture
plonked in the path of traditional flyways
that trace a bigger and older picture
than any painting on any wall.

2 A model of comportment

Water is a leveller for swans.
This calming river named in their honour
keeps them side by side, attired
in modest black. Nothing hierarchical,
no jostling for pre-eminence. Flatly
egalitarian, they mind their placid business
and glide along with easy-going feet
except for an occasional discreet
moan of mild contentment.

Couldn't be more different from the white
mob of corellas nearby, incessantly raucous,
restless, competing for the topmost branch,
shoving each other aside with feathered elbows
and indignant shrieks of *me me me
position position position I'm up, you're down.*
Reminds you of certain former colleagues – who
would probably say you were a squabbler too
and may be right about that.

Today it's this dark flotilla of swans
that you admire, their dealings with each other
serenely horizontal, their individual posture
upright, disdaining any rowdiness,
with nobody either in front or left behind.
Who's in charge here? Which one's the admiral?
The issue doesn't arise. They move without haste
or deference. If only you, displaced,
could apply somehow to join them…

Bathos at Balyang

Back then, before 'outing' became a term
of disclosure, it meant a pleasurable excursion,
such as a family picnic. For us, those occasions
must have been frequent, though not much stays
in my mind, except for part of one day:
snagged on memory's wire is a fragment
of an outing to Balyang wetlands, paradise
for waterbirds and watchers.

We stretched our legs and slouched beside a pond
for a balmy hour or so, idly observing
a pair of pelicans, portly, with pouched throats
cold eyes and quite preposterous beaks
glide snootily past us in a fake display
of dignity, posturing as paragons of style.
Mildly comic, this regal affectation –
but hilarity followed when an uncouth relative
descended clumsily towards the lake,
veering on wobblesome wings, all elbows
and waggly undercarriage, to make a rude
embarrassed hash of a splashdown.
As its midriff hit the water, my young
daughter yelped with delight, 'Bellywhacker!'
and went on chortling at this disparity
between the stiff manner of the gliding pair
and the arrival of their graceless cousin.
Her laughter was purer, more luminous
than any sound I heard from her thereafter.

I hope it lingered with her a long while,
that moment of sheer merriment when
a maladroit disrupter, ungainly as a clown,
appalled his fellow Balyang pelicans
by bellywhacking down.

Perhaps she glimpsed something more, sensing
in that stumblebum way of going to water a token
of my parental double act: the pretence
of coolness marred by a foolish propensity
for coming a whopping cropper.

My migrant way of moving

I hadn't given it a thought in years,
this distant relic of a deadened childhood.
Suddenly here's a lively pastoral
specimen rambling across a grassy field
in an Instagram post from Danish friends.

Startling to see it looks so much at home
in a Scandi setting instead of the British one –
which I'd supposed was this shy creature's true
habitat, a Beatrix Potter landscape
criss-crossed hospitably by hedgerows,

though I'd got to know it in a different place
far from England or Denmark: the one country
that introduced it (a British settler's whim)
and saw it become prolific, more so than in
its native lands on the other side of the world.

At dawn I'd leave a saucer of milk-soaked bits
of bread on the lawn and watch from a window
as it shuffled towards breakfast, sniffing,
dawdling along as if still puzzled by
its transportation, an involuntary expat.

The hedgehog, knowing just a single thing,
is a stickler for doing it well (Archilochus).
Nudge its flank, it'll turn into a globe,
bristling with spikes like a virus parody,
and then slowly uncurl to set off again –

perfect exemplar of my migrant way
of moving: no nonchalant *flâneur* but
wary, tentative, cautiously ready
to resort to that one trick, a defensive
roll into a ball of temporary prickles.

Archilochus, a Greek lyric poet of the seventh century BC, is known mainly through fragments such as his aphorism contrasting the fox, who knows many things, with the hedgehog, who knows a single good one.

Being loved to bits

Blame Lewis Carroll: most of us can't think
of a white rabbit without envisaging
the pocket watch, the fuss, the anxious haste,
the running-late for an urgent rendezvous.

Crouched in a corner of my memory
is a different creature, just as white
and every inch a rabbit, but a pet,
cohabiting quietly with a guinea pig.

In a spacious hutch they hung out together,
companionable as confirmed bachelors
and gourmet nibblers, watched intently
by my young daughter, who duly reported

that eating, resting, cuddling were their sole
pursuits – until the day when she came running
anguished into the house: catastrophe
had struck. 'Our guinea pig has come to bits!'

Agog, I rushed outside, imagining
a hand grenade, a fox, a rabid rabbit –
only to find the guinea pig was not
as masculine as we'd been told. Lounging

on every side were newly minted babies,
superintended by their proud producer
and beamed at by their fat white foster uncle
who wasn't in a hurry to go anywhere.

The cat's whiskers

Cradling a creature as its last breath leaves
a flimsy worn-out body
is something you never forget;

but less dismal moments linger still
in the curious cabinet of memory,
helping to soften regret:

on the windowsill close to my pillow
there will always remain faint
scratch-marks where paws used to land

soundlessly, before she'd step across
to tickle my face with mischievous
whiskery kisses. My missing friend.

Turnings

Season of mystic metamorphoses,
of shifted sets, old shapes expunged,
switched-colour outfits rearranged,
when there's no turncoat more bizarre than these:

a crowd of mutant crested cockatoos,
their bodies thinned to slender stalks,
their clownish heads like gaudy jokes,
faces all flushed, with startled green hairdos.

Give them a second glance, and they'll appear
in quite another guise: dressed so
like florid marsupial mitts – presto!
Let's think of it as Ovid's time of year,

when this converts to that, and that in turn
to something else… But how it'll all
turn out – ah, there's a different tale!
Climate awry? Then must our emperor spurn

the poet of transformations, turn him out
of home into a cold exile?
No further spring beyond the pale?
Last post for Ceres? Not a seed of doubt?

Or can the quick-change artist yet improve
our lot by cultivating tropes
to freshen an empire's faded hopes
of turning a corner – so we all survive?

Reciprocal mysteries

The countless feathered corpses: why
do we seldom see any of them? Where
do all those birds go to die? On a day
as fiercely hot as this, scorching the air,
there's not a single avian note,
not a chirp, quick cheep or squawk
or even any clearing of the throat,
though I know winged things do lurk
in garden crannies, wherever they're able
to shelter behind shady walls
and if one of them, stricken, falls
from its hiding place, dead as a pebble,
who carries it away?

Birds, we guess, have no funeral rites,
no mourning period, no sting of
sorrow, no memory of lost mates.
Perhaps we're wrong. Their lilting lingo,
arcane to us – could it distil grief?
This morning's magpie trill, filling
our backyard at first light – what if
it was an elegy for the fallen?
Which of us can say?

Might birds, for their part, feel a sense
of puzzlement about where we go
finally, supposing humans show
no sign of grief, sing no laments,
but silently,
invisibly,
just get carried away?

In a darkening shade

Now, more and more, she feels her days
are leaking colour, losing shape.
There's no reprieve, nor any escape
from the approaching final phase.

A gradual ebbing of her sight
isn't the sole diminishment.
She wonders where her vigour went
and why she's restless through the night.

For some years now she's been alone.
From time to time he'll cross her mind
but bit by bit she's grown resigned
to living quietly on her own,

the sole custodian of her plight.
Friendships have simply lapsed somehow.
The garden brings her solace now
despite the waning of the light.

A seat's well placed so she can peer
into the trees where small birds flit
and though she makes out some of it
fine details are no longer clear.

Having landscaped it all, she's proud
of nooks and flowerbeds she once made
but as she watches them, things fade
and blur like distant wisps of cloud.

Yet resonance remains. The song
of honeyeaters rides the breeze
and blossoms are abuzz because
bees pleasure them all summer long.

Parading in their party hats,
pert parrots verge on parody,
with no pretence at melody
as they engage in strident spats.

Loudmouth crows are bully boys,
magpies are comparing notes,
there's no catch in froggy throats –
the whole shebang is full of noise.

But as the sun slides to the west,
their raucousness subsides, and peace
enters the garden. Her release
approaches gently, taps her wrist.

Eyes close. Her pulse slows to a crawl
like music with a dying fall.
She smiles at hearing, last of all,
a honeyeater's feeding call.

I chose here the strict verse form of iambic tetrameter lines set in quatrains rhymed abba because it follows the example of a famous poem of the Victorian period, Tennyson's 'In Memoriam', which established a strong link between this particular taut verse pattern and an elegiac theme. As 'In Memoriam' mentions birdsong more than a score of times, mostly in a consoling tone, it came to mind when I was beginning to think about the subject of my own composition.

Filth into growth

'Vernal' isn't enough. On its own, an upswing
of the eternal wheel, massive and lumbering,
couldn't produce such a pageant of rebirth
enacted on branch after branch after branch –
this age-old miracle play of green-tip growth
as miniature hands no longer tightly clenched
gently uncurl their tentative fingers:
it all takes more than the mere coming of spring.

It takes detritus too, and the whole unhurried
process of darkly decomposing matter.
It takes thick humus, built from a scattering
of husks, twiggage, leafage, tattered or florid,
lingersome dreck and mould, and underneath
a stockpile of rotting bodily bits: the soundless
biotic ritual of slowly breaking down
whatever may fall on the digestive earth.

Bushland or backyard garden, it's much the same:
from the foul the fresh unfolds. Bedraggled blooms
sloughed by shrubs, discarded peels and cores,
those grub-drilled cabbages, wrinkled citrus rinds,
accumulated scraps, shreds and slops,
the wilt, the muck, surprising raked-up finds –
into the messy compost it all pours,
making lavish potage to feed later crops.

From this litter of leavings and lapsed vegetables,
from so many drooping dropping dying things,
such nourishment, filthy rich, can spring
it's enough to render us humble, since humility
means being grounded deep and firm in the soil
– an undertaking to which at last we'll bring
our own small offerings, the modest spoil
of transitory selves, biodegradable.

De profundis

All deep things are Song. It seems
the very central essence of us, Song.
As if all the rest were but wrappages and hulls.
– Thomas Carlyle

Some beings can't long survive
above the surface.
Some singing belongs in the depths,
spreading and sinking fathoms down.

Those mesmeric siren sounds, making
timbers of old ships tremble and ache
with love, were voiced by wandering
cetacean minstrels. Hearing them could
capsize your heart.
Easier to stop up your ears, to reach
for harpoons, flensing knives, and then
try not to listen to the massive lungs
releasing wistfully a last soft breath
like whispered memory, in one slow hiss.

Mutely commemorating their deep music
is what you see here suspended overhead,
this museum's proudest drawcard:
a vast bone-slatted cavern that encloses
emptiness and a long blaring silence.

Acknowledgements

Some of these poems have appeared in *Antipodes, Epoch, Nantucket Review* and *Shot Glass* (USA), *Ariel* and *Descant* (Canada), *Catalyst, Climate* and *Flash Frontier* (New Zealand), and in the Australian magazines *Burrow, Cordite, Creatrix, Mattoid, Meanjin, Pure Slush, Quadrant, Saltbush Review, StylusLit, South-West Review, Unlikely* and *Voices*.

Others have been anthologised in *Alarm & Longing, Brushstrokes, Ear to Earth, Hope, Mapped But Not Known, Neither Nuked nor Crucified, Number 2 Friendly Street, Out of the Shadows, Pattern and Voice, Play, Poetry d'Amour, Poetry Downtown, Poetry for the Planet, Shorelines, Sonnets on Western Australia, The Friendly Street Poetry Reader, Tuesday Night Live* and *Writings from the Shipwreck Coast*.

Thanks are due to the editors of all those publications for their support, and also to the judges of competitions in which a few of my poems have won awards or shortlistings/commendations (the Antipodes Prize, Henry Kendall Prize, Joanne Burns Award, Letter Review Prize, Mundaring Prize, Poetry d'Amour Prize, ACU Prize, Alice Sinclair Prize, Shakespeare Society Prize, Mattara Prize).

Several poems, or earlier versions, appeared in my books *Rhumbs, Undercover Agent* and *The Shifting Shore*. Since then I have revised most of them.

I am glad to record here my gratitude to a number of fellow poets whose example and encouragement helped me to develop a clearer sense of my craft. At a neophyte stage I learned much from the generosity of Lauris Edmond, Denise Levertov and Judith Wright; I wish they were still alive so that I could give each of them a copy of this book. Others to whom I'm also indebted in various ways (more than some of them may be aware) include Brian Edwards, Robyn Gardner, Dennis Haskell, Barry Hill, Elizabeth Smither and Andrew Taylor. Above all I want to thank Gale MacLachlan for her steady personal support of my writing over a long period.

About the author

Ian Reid grew up in New Zealand and lived briefly in the USA but for many years his home has been in Perth, Western Australia. His poems appear internationally in various literary magazines and anthologies. Book-length selections of his poetry have been published in Australia, Canada and the USA. He is also the author of a dozen books in other genres, including five novels. Among his awards is the Antipodes prize for poetry, and his writings are translated into five foreign languages.

Ian has worked as a teacher of literature and creative writing in several institutions, a university administrator, a consultant for organisations across all sectors, a manuscript assessor for numerous publishers, a CEO of Leadership WA, a director of the Australian Society of Authors, a peer reviewer for the Australia Council, and head judge of the WA Premier's Book Awards. He is an Adjunct Professor in English and Literary Studies at the University of Western Australia. His website 'Reid on Writing' is at http://ianreid-author.com

www.ingramcontent.com/pod-product-compliance
Lightning Source LLC
Chambersburg PA
CBHW070949080526
44587CB00015B/2236